NORTH AMERICAN
FORTS
AND
FORTIFICATIONS

by

Michelle M. Pangallo

CAMBRIDGE UNIVERSITY PRESS
Cambridge
London   New York   New Rochelle
Melbourne   Sydney

CONTENTS

FORTS AND FORTIFICATIONS

What is a fort? The word itself literally means "a strong place."
The purpose of a strong place is to provide defense against
enemy attack.

All living creatures have a basic need to protect themselves
from things and forces that threaten their well-being. Nature
has equipped animals with various means to help them survive.
Turtle shells, porcupine quills and moose antlers are all
examples of natural defenses.

Human beings, as well, have an inborn need to place
barriers between themselves and unfriendly intruders. Man has
had to use his intellect to help him devise ways to fend off his
foes. This art of designing and building works for defense is
called fortification.

In very primitive times, the wall served as a key source of
protection for the peoples of the world. From this simple
structure, fortification has grown into the complex defense
systems of modern society.

Forts have played a major role in the development of
North America. Hundreds of historical forts dot the United
States and Canada today. Some are well preserved; some have
faded into the past; but all have a story to tell.

CASTILLO DE SAN MARCOS

The brilliant white walls and red watchtowers of Castillo de San Marcos have faded over the centuries but this somber fortress at the water's edge still dominates the oldest city in the continental United States, St Augustine. This city lies on a narrow peninsula on Florida's eastern coast and faces the Matanzas River. A national monument, the Castillo is an excellent reminder of America's early Spanish history.

When the French established a settlement at the mouth of St John's River in northern Florida in 1564, they named it Fort Caroline after their teenage king, Charles. Upon learning of the French fort in the New World, King Philip II of Spain became quite furious. He felt that the French were trespassing on Spanish property. He promptly sent Don Pedro Menendez de Aviles, Captain-General of the Spanish treasure fleet, to wipe out the colony and thus protect the Spanish claim to Florida. The king was also eager to prevent pirate raids on Spanish galleons as they sailed along the wild coasts of Florida while following the Gulf Stream, the shortest route from the New World to the Old. Laden with gold and silver from the mines of Peru and New Spain (Mexico), these vessels carried untold riches back to Spain.

So, in 1565, fifty-five years before the Pilgrims landed at Plymouth, Menendez stepped ashore onto land claimed earlier by Spanish explorer Ponce de Leon. Menendez and his men quickly set about fortifying this colony they called St Augustine. A few days later, French ships, led by the bold captain Jean Ribault, loomed into view. However, before the French fleet could swarm in and attack St Augustine, blustering winds scattered and wrecked the ships far down the coast. Snatching the moment, Menendez marched his men through drenching rains and swampy lands to capture the undermanned Fort Caroline. The Spaniards easily overtook the fort and massacred nearly all of its 150 defenders. Not one Spanish life was lost.

In a grisly turn of events, Ribault and his soldiers who had survived the shipwrecks, were taken prisoner by Menendez and his men. They were mercilessly put to death. The Spanish fort that was later built on these blood-soaked sands was aptly named Matanzas, the Spanish word for slaughters.

Spain kept its hold on the American continent. Over the next 100 years, nine earth and wooden forts were constructed one after another to protect St Augustine. Enemy raids, foul weather, fires, termites and time itself took their toll on these crudely built forts. A pirate attack in 1668 and the English settlement of Charleston, a little more than 200 miles (320 km) to the north of St Augustine, convinced Queen Mariana of Spain that a strong and durable fortification was sorely needed.

Ignacio Daza, a military engineer, drew the plan for the fort, Castillo de San Marcos in 1672. It was completed 23 years later in 1695. This fort served not only as a defense against attack but also as a citadel or huge shelter for the people of St Augustine.

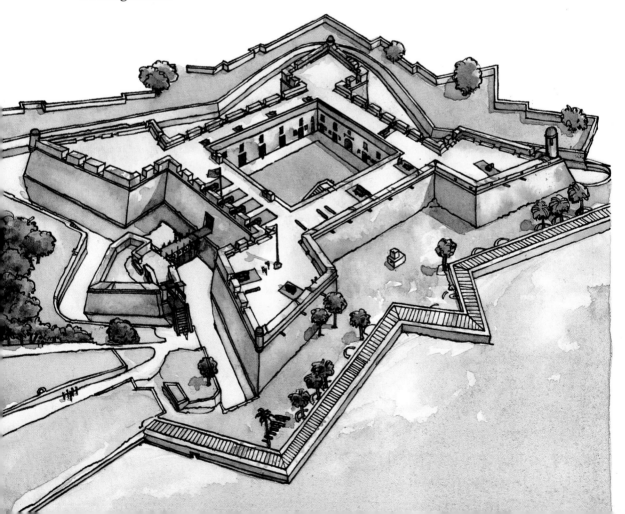

Remarkably, this mighty stronghold was built of seashells. The Spanish used a substance called coquina (ko KEE na) found on an island across the bay, Anastasia Island. Coquina is a rock made up of broken seashells stuck together over a long period of time by their own lime. Indian and Spanish workers quarried the coquina, ferried it to the building site, and then cut it into blocks. The fort's walls, 13 feet (4 meters) thick were to vex many attacking cannoneers. Cannon balls could not splinter the soft shellstone! The iron balls simply bounced off or were absorbed.

Basically, the fortress was square in design with a large pointed projection, called a bastion, at each corner. A tidal moat surrounded the massive structure. The dirt dug out of the moat was used to make a slope or hill called a glacis. Attackers had to move up this embankment so they were exposed to fire from the fort. The fort also had a hot shot furnace which heated cannon balls red hot. They could then set ships on fire as well as smash them.

The Castillo was besieged numerous times but never taken. In 1763, the fort finally fell into British hands when Spain traded Florida for Havana, Cuba. During the American

Revolution, the British Redcoats used the Castillo as a prison for American "rebels." By treaty, at the War's end, Britain returned Florida to Spain. Owning Florida became a burden to Spain so in 1821 Spain ceded Florida to the United States.

To honor General Francis Marion, the "Swamp Fox" of the Revolutionary War, the United States renamed the Castillo, Fort Marion. Under the American flag, the fort served as a military prison for Indians. The Seminoles, Apaches and Plains Indians were all imprisoned there at different times. Wildcat, the Seminole leader, led a daring escape from the fort.

Confederate soldiers occupied the fort for a short while during the Civil War. After the Spanish–American War, it no longer played an active military role.

 In 1942 Congress restored the fort's original name, Castillo de San Marcos. Today the Castillo, America's oldest masonry fort, is a part of the National Park Service of the United States and is preserved for the benefit of the people.

FORT TICONDEROGA

In 1755 the French built a mighty fortress on a point of land which the Indians called Ticonderoga, or "between big waters." They named their fort Carillon, meaning "chimes of bells," because of the musical sounds of the nearby falls. This four-bastioned fort commanded the narrows where Lake George empties into Lake Champlain.

People travelled by water in colonial North America because few roads had been built. Rivers and lakes served as highways for both trade and war. The only practical route between Canada and the British colonies was through the narrows at Ticonderoga. Whoever held this fort controlled an essential waterway. It is clear to see why Ticonderoga was called the "Key to a Continent."

Canadian Governor Vaudreuil chose Lieutenant Michel Chartier, Sieur de Lotbinière, a young engineer officer, to build a fort in the wilderness of Ticonderoga. Even though he had never been in battle, de Lotbinière knew the importance of a strong fort. His plan copied closely the forts of Vauban, the French master military engineer. For the main walls, he used heavy oak timbers placed horizontally one on top of another and filled behind with dirt and rubble. There were two such log walls ten feet (three meters) apart and fastened to each other with cross timbers dovetailed in place. These walls presented the best defense against artillery but were not permanent because the wood rotted. In 1757 de Lotbinière began to substitute stone for the timber on the outer walls to make the fort more durable.

During the French and Indian War, the capture of Carillon, the strongest of the French forts on Lake Champlain, became an important goal to the British. William Pitt, the Prime Minister of England, commanded Major-General James Abercrombie to attack the fort.

Unfortunately, Abercrombie was a weak leader. In fact, he had so much trouble making up his mind that behind his back his soldiers called him "Mrs Namby Crombie" and his officers called him "Aunt Abby." It is not surprising then that the shrewd William Pitt placed Lord Howe as second in command. Howe was a brilliant soldier and adored by those he led. With Howe to advise Abercrombie, the British were sure of victory at Fort Carillon.

On the morning of July 5, 1758, the English army set sail on the sparkling blue waters of Lake George. What a spectacular sight it was! Nearly 15,000 men floated down the lake in almost 900 little boats, 135 whaleboats and a large number of flatboats carrying artillery. The column of crafts, filled with red coats and the plaids of Highlanders, was more than 6 miles (10 km) long. It was the finest army yet seen in North America.

Inside the fort, the French General Montcalm kept a cool head. Even though he knew he was outnumbered four to one, he did not plan to lose the fort. He ordered his men to build a huge long wall on the ridge some distance from the fort. The wall zig-zagged so that the French soldiers could shoot the attackers from many angles. In front of the wall, a big trench was dug. The land leading up to the trench was scattered with trees, boughs and tangled brush. General Montcalm hoped that Abercrombie would be foolish enough to send his men into this trap. They would be easy targets.

Fate was to grant Montcalm his wish. A French bullet felled Lord Howe as he advanced toward Carillon. The British army was terribly saddened by his death. They knew that Abercrombie was unfit to lead them alone. He proved them right.

Without even waiting for his cannons to be hauled up, Abercrombie commanded his men to charge the fort. They became tangled in the heaps of branches and quickly met their doom. Almost 3,000 men were lost before the British were forced to retreat and concede defeat to the French who lost only a few hundred men. It was indeed a black day for the British!

The ancient Roman saying "Sic transit gloria mundi" (All glory is fleeting) proved apt for the French. The next year another great English army commanded by Lord Jeffrey Amherst succeeded in capturing Carillon after a four-day siege. The French, whose Indian allies were quickly fading away, set fire to the fort before abandoning it to the British. The main walls of the fort were not badly damaged. The British made the necessary repairs and renamed the fort Ticonderoga. While the red, white and blue Union flag fluttered in the breeze, a small garrison kept watch over the fort for the next sixteen years.

"The shot heard round the world" at Lexington and Concord, two little Massachusetts villages, shattered the peaceful stillness at Ticonderoga in 1775. The American Revolution had begun. Once again the seizure of strong Fort Ticonderoga became important. This time it was the colonists who wanted to capture the large quantity of military supplies stored in the fort.

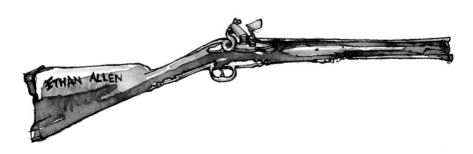

An expedition led by Benedict Arnold and Ethan Allen set out to take Fort Ti from the British Redcoats. Without spilling any blood, they were able to surprise the sleeping British in their nightshirts and force them to surrender. The Americans held the fort until July 1777, when General John Burgoyne easily chased them away. In October 1777, the fort was abandoned. Except for a brief British occupation in 1780–81, it was never garrisoned again.

 The fort has been ably and faithfully restored through the efforts of the late Stephen H. P. Pell and the Fort Ticonderoga Association and now stands as an historic monument to the brave men of three nations who served their countries there.

THE FORTRESS
OF LOUISBOURG

A time machine is not necessary for a journey into the past.
Parks Canada has made it possible to experience life as it once
was in the eighteenth-century fortified town of Louisbourg.
Once inside the Dauphin Gate, visitors can mingle with
soldiers and townspeople clad in period costume. Next they
can explore colonial buildings and even sample such
eighteenth-century style foods as hearty fish pies and warm
brown bread. All of these encounters help to shed more light
on the saga of Louisbourg.

By the Treaty of Utrecht, 1713, which ended the War of Spanish Succession, France lost nearly all of Newfoundland and Acadia (mainland Nova Scotia) to Britain. She was left with only Cape Breton Island and Prince Edward Island in the Gulf of St Lawrence. To guard the approaches to the St Lawrence River and to protect her dwindling possessions in North America, France began to build a huge and costly fortified town at Louisbourg. Set upon the rugged rocks of the eastern tip of Cape Breton Island, Louisbourg was a very sound choice. It had a large harbor that did not freeze and it was quite close to the profitable cod fishery of the Grand Banks.

The windswept beaches of Louisbourg soon bustled with the activities of the sea. Ruddy-cheeked fishermen hauled their plentiful catches ashore. There they split, salted and hung the codfish on racks to dry. After the fish were dried, they were loaded on ships for transport to European markets. Then as now, codfish was a vital source of food for the peoples of the world.

The settlement at Louisbourg also prospered as a trading center. Rivalling Boston, Philadelphia and New York, Louisbourg thrived as a trans-shipping point between the old world and the new. The snug inlet welcomed trading vessels from the West Indies, France, New England and Canada. Cargo ships put in to port with supplies and luxury goods for the colonies. These same ships scudded home laden with rum, sugar and molasses from the Indies and dried fish from the North Atlantic. Meanwhile, Louisbourg merchants grew rich trading French wines and dainty lace with New England for staples and building materials. It was in this way that Louisbourg boomed as a sort of world warehouse.

Unfortunately for Louisbourg, trading with the enemy had definite drawbacks. The same New Englanders who bartered, bought and sold inside the fort's walls later returned to attack it! Supposedly, the massive fortress was impregnable but upon close inspection, the New England tradesmen noted many glaring weaknesses.

The fortress badly needed repairs and more cannons. The garrison grumbled loudly about the lack of supplies. But above all, the basic Vauban design of the fort itself, that of stone bastions and outlying defenses, was riddled with flaws! Some points were left unfortified and others were commanded by

CONGE N.º 240
D'UN AN

POUR LA PESCHE DU POISSON FRAIS AUX ISLES.

OUIS-JEAN-MARIE DE BOURBON, DUC DE PENTHIEVRE, DE CHATEAU-VILAIN, ET DE RAMBOUILLET, Amiral de France, Gouverneur & Lieutenant-General pour le Roy en sa Province de Bretagne. A TOUS ceux qui ces présentes Lettres verront, SALUT. Sçavoir faisons, que Nous avons donné Congé & Permission à *nommé François Labée* — Maistre du Bastiment François nommé *la cidienne* du port de

pourrier premier mil sept cent *quarante trois* en vertu du certificat de M. *L.D.g.* de l'amirauté *Retiré* retiré l'ancien Congé & *l'ancien Congé n.º 174* reçu pour ledit Congé

andré Parerot p. *vue monpure*

higher ground. Despite more than two decades of construction at great expense, King Louis XV's imposing stronghold proved to be a failure.

In May 1745 with France and England again at war, an expedition of New England volunteers carried by British ships laid siege to Louisbourg. After seven weeks, the garrison surrendered and the fortress fell. However, the victors had little time to revel in their achievement. For just three years later, the British signed the Treaty of Aix-la-Chapelle which gave Louisbourg back to the French. This stroke of the pen greatly irked the New Englanders who were already beginning to question British policies.

The French tried earnestly to strengthen the fortifications but to little purpose. They were still unable to hold the fort when the British launched a second assault in the summer of 1759. Under the dashing leadership of Brigadier General James Wolfe, a British force of 16,000 troops and 150 ships battered Louisbourg's same weak spots. The French defenders, merchants as well as soldiers, fought valiantly but after seven weeks were forced to lay down their arms. To their chagrin, history had repeated itself.

This time, however, the British were bent on keeping the French from ever having another chance to regain their prize. They decided to demolish Louisbourg completely. Skilled engineers blasted the mighty fortress into masses of rubble. Although it remained in ruins for two centuries, the world had not heard the last of Louisbourg.

In 1961 Canada started a 25 million dollar project to reconstruct one quarter of the Fortress of Louisbourg. The government wanted to provide work for Cape Breton's jobless coal miners and to preserve a colorful chapter in Canadian history. Through archaeological excavation and careful research, Louisbourg has once again come to life.

OPPOSITE: 'Licence for a year for catching fish in Island waters' granted to Francois Labée by the governor, and a photograph of the Fortress of Louisbourg today.

FORT McHENRY

Star is a key word in the history of Fort McHenry. Not only was this famous fort built in the shape of a star but also it was the scene of a bombardment which inspired the writing of "The Star-Spangled Banner." Indeed, Fort McHenry played one of the star roles in the shaping of America's heritage.

In all likelihood, there is no better-known coastal fort than Fort McHenry in Maryland. Hastily built of earthen mounds on Whetstone Point in 1776, it was originally named Fort Whetstone. Fearing a British attack, the citizens of Baltimore made a wise decision when they constructed a fort on Whetstone Point, a body of land surrounded by water on three sides. This peninsular location was ideal to aid them in guarding the approaches to Baltimore from the Patapsco River and the Chesapeake Bay.

Even though the British never did attack Baltimore during the Revolutionary War, no one ever doubted the merit of this seacoast fortification on Whetstone Point. In 1794 Congress voted in favor of erecting fortifications to protect important cities along the Atlantic coast. Secretary of War, James McHenry, citizen of Baltimore, helped his fellow Marylanders raise money for the costly project. The fort was later renamed Fort McHenry in his honor.

Famous Fort McHenry was completed around 1800. Its form was that of a five-pointed star. Military engineers favored this five-bastioned pentagon shape during the late eighteenth century. This plan made it possible for soldiers to see and cover by fire all portions of the wall from some other portion of the wall.

Fort McHenry was a solid fort. Both the inside and outside of the fort's dirt walls were faced with brick. Within the star fort were barracks, a guardhouse and a powder magazine. A ditch surrounding the fort and a V-shaped embankment (ravelin) in front of the entrance were added later.

From 1793 to 1815 France and Great Britain were at war

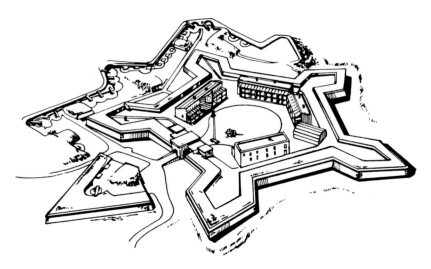

with each other. To keep supplies from reaching their enemies, both sides seized American cargoes and merchant ships. Also, the British tactic of capturing American seamen and forcing them to serve in the Royal Navy greatly angered the United States. On June 18, 1812, Congress declared war on Great Britain.

The rich port city of Baltimore became a center for privateering. Privateers were privately owned ships that the government permitted to capture British merchant ships. Naturally, this practice fanned the flames of British bitterness toward America.

In the mean time, expecting to be the target of British revenge, the spirited citizens of Baltimore carefully prepared their defenses. Working parties dug trenches and erected fortifications around the city. They knew that the British called their beloved city a "nest of pirates" and would stop at nothing to crush it.

When news of the British pillaging and burning of Washington reached Baltimore, people realized that it was just a matter of time before they, too, faced attack. Three groups of defenders, the United States Army Corps of Artillery, the Maryland Militia and sailors from Commodore Joshua Barney's Flotilla, stood ready with guns and ammunition to defend Fort McHenry. Thousands more manned the works around the city.

No one was surprised when in September of 1814 British vessels, commanded by Admiral Cochrane, sailed into Balti-

more Harbor and began their bombardment. Under the
command of Major Armistead, the 1,000 men inside the fort
soon found out that their shot and shell fell short of the
enemy. The clever British had anchored just out of range of the
fort's guns! Equipped with long-range guns, the British steadily
hurled rockets and mortar shells at Fort McHenry. Inside the
fort, the Americans waited silently and somewhat impatiently.
At last their chance to return fire came when the British tried
to come in closer for an attack. Through rain, darkness and
the smoke of battle, Major Armistead's courageous soldiers
fired their cannons at the attackers.

As Francis Scott Key, a prominent lawyer, watched the
constant bombardment of Fort McHenry, he was filled with
anxiety. He was being held by the British on board the sloop,
Minden, about 4 miles (6 km) from shore. He had set out to
seek the release of his friend, Dr Beanes, who was a British
captive.

In the pale light of dawn, Francis Scott Key's worried eyes
surveyed the horizon. After twenty-five hours, the British had
finally ceased their attack. They had withdrawn their fleet! To
his enormous relief, Francis Scott Key spotted the broad stripes
and bright stars of the great garrison flag. The huge woolen
banner was battered but still waved defiantly over the fort.
Baltimore was saved! Overcome with joy, Key dashed off the

words to a poem on the back of an envelope he took from his pocket. This poem was later set to music and became "The Star-Spangled Banner," America's national anthem. The garrison flag had earned a special place in American history. It was one of the biggest banners ever made in America—it was 30 feet (9 meters) wide and 42 feet (13 meters) long—and was sewn by a woman, Mary Pickersgill of Baltimore. It is now on display in the Smithsonian Institution in Washington, DC.

After the Battle of Baltimore, Fort McHenry saw no more fighting. During the Civil War, it was used as a prison for Confederate soldiers and political prisoners. It later served as a military hospital for injured servicemen during World War I.

☆
☆
☆
☆ In 1925, Fort McHenry was made a
☆ national park. Today, the National Park
☆ Service operates the park as a national
☆ monument and historic shrine. By
☆ presidential proclamation, the fort has the
☆ special privilege granted to only a few
☆ places to fly the American flag for twenty-
   four hours a day.

OLD FORT HENRY

At the end of the American Revolution, not all colonists were pleased to have won their independence from the Crown. Many felt strongly that they should remain loyal to Great Britain. Called Loyalists, they left their homes forever and headed for what remained of British North America. Some settled at King's Town or Kingston where the St Lawrence River begins to flow out of Lake Ontario. With hard work and determination, these refugees adjusted quickly to their new lives in Upper Canada.

In 1812, gathering war clouds prompted the hasty construction of a fort to guard Kingston harbor. Built of logs and earth, it contained a large battery to cover the water approach. Despite the fact that the Americans never did attack Kingston during the War of 1812, the British feared they might not be so lucky in the future. Mindful of Kingston's strategic importance as a military and naval headquarters and as a hive of shipbuilding activity, the British made plans to fortify the area. Even the famed Duke of Wellington was concerned. In 1819, he wrote "...there must be a good fort at Point Henry."

And a good fort there was to be. The old wooden fort was dismantled. In its place on that rocky high point of land rose a grand structure. Built of native limestone, the main work was a casemated six-sided fortification set into the hill. The flanking ditches were wide and deep and could be covered by guns on the ramparts. The only entrance to the fort was by draw-bridge. In addition, nearly every room in the fort had one to three small openings in the wall through which small arms could be fired. These tiny windows were called loopholes.

Because Fort Henry's main armament faced inland, some people thought that the fort had been built backwards! However, it was not folly but foresight that inspired this design. The planners of the fort knew that American forces would never be witless enough to venture into Kingston harbor under the watchful eye of the British Navy. Instead they could simply slip ashore where there were miles of undefended shoreline. Quite wisely, the defenders of Fort Henry were prepared for an attack by land.

But it was an attack that never came. Fort Henry had proved to be a powerful deterrent. Its very presence had daunted the enemy!

By 1890, the fort had outlived its usefulness and was abandoned. In the late 1930s the Federal and Provincial governments restored the fort to its original state.

Today the Fort Henry Guard, a specially trained group of Canadian high school, college and university students "garrison" Old Fort Henry. With their well-tended goat mascot, David, they do a splendid job of reenacting military life in 1867. Visitors can watch a thrilling display of infantry drills and artillery salutes. The scarlet-clad Guard does mock field battle in long red lines, the famous Thin Red Line formation. To show a cavalry attack, they rally to position to form the British Square. The urgent rattle of drums and the shrill tones of the fife give coded messages to the troops in battle. A cannonade thunders through the pepper-colored haze swirling lazily over the parade-ground. Spectators are not likely to forget these sights and sounds of battle.

FORT SUMTER

The glowing cannonball hurled its way through the soft gray mist of dawn on April 12, 1861. The Confederate troops commanded by General P.G.T. Beauregard had made good their threat. Fort Sumter in South Carolina had been fired upon!

Fort Sumter was a five-sided brick fort which stood on a man-made island above the deep waters of Charleston Harbor. This fort was one of a series of seacoast fortifications built by the United States after the War of 1812. It was named for South Carolina's Revolutionary War hero, General Thomas Sumter.

After South Carolina left the Union followed by Texas, Louisiana, Mississippi, Alabama, Georgia and Florida to form the Confederate States of America, most Southerners felt that this fort should belong to them and not to the United States Government. They thought that United States troops should not be within Confederate borders. The United States, however, did not agree!

Confederate commissioners went to Washington to try to arrange a peaceful withdrawal of the United States troops. Since neither side would give in, an agreement could not be reached. The distant drums of war began to beat louder.

One dark December night, Major Robert Anderson, who had been occupying nearby Fort Moultrie, led his small garrison of Union soldiers across the channel into Fort Sumter. He and his little group of men, less than one hundred in all, set about to defend the approach by sea to the city of Charleston.

Completely surprised by Anderson's actions, the Confederates became outraged. They clamored for action. And so it was with great support that General Beauregard commanded his Carolina forces to aim their artillery toward three sides of Sumter.

Major Anderson faced many difficult problems. Even though construction of Fort Sumter had begun in 1829, it had

just been essentially completed that year. The structure was so new that only 60 cannons were mounted despite the fact that the fort was designed for 135 guns. Food supplies were low. There was only enough flour, hard bread, rice, sugar, coffee, salt, salt pork, hominy grits and corn meal to last a short while. If the Yankee ships carrying provisions did not arrive in time, Major Anderson knew that he and his men would be facing yet another foe—hunger. Nevertheless, he bravely refused to give up the fort to General Beauregard.

Although tempers grew as hot as molten ash, Beauregard and Anderson were very courteous at all times. They sent many messages to each other and despite their vast differences of opinion, they wrote in a gentlemanly manner. In fact, Beauregard even told Anderson the exact time that he was going to fire on Fort Sumter.

People who had come from miles around by buggy, by train and on foot into Charleston that April morning, cheered heartily as the first iron ball arched across the harbor. This shot was the first of almost three thousand more which were to bombard Fort Sumter.

Inside the fort Major Anderson's tired and hungry men tried as best they could to battle the smoke and flames. The United States ships carrying food and supplies were chased back out to sea by the Confederates. Now the men would surely starve. So as their blue uniforms grew dustier, all hopes of keeping the fort grew dimmer. At the end of the second day's fight, Major Anderson surrendered Fort Sumter. Amazingly, there had been no loss of life on either side.

After firing a 50-gun salute to the Stars and Stripes, which sadly resulted in an explosion that caused the death of two Union soldiers, Major Anderson marched his small garrison out of Fort Sumter onto a steamer to the tune of "Yankee Doodle." The victorious Southerners who watched them leave did not cheer but rather removed their hats and bowed their heads as a sign of respect.

On Monday morning, April 15, President Lincoln issued a proclamation calling for 75,000 troops. Northerners eagerly responded. War! Nothing now could stop it. The bombardment of Fort Sumter had signalled the start of the Civil War. A war so horrible that brothers would fight brothers.

For nearly four years, the Confederate flag remained over Charleston Harbor. The Union's first attempt to recapture Fort Sumter on April 7, 1863 ended in failure. A fleet of nine ironclad warships led by Rear Admiral Samuel F. du Pont proved no match against such a solid fort. While Fort Sumter suffered little damage, one Union ship was sunk and the others were terribly battered.

In August, determined Union troops began a heavy bombardment of Fort Sumter. As the artillery shattered the fort's masonry walls, Confederate soldiers quickly rebuilt them with dirt, sand and bales of cotton. Federal shots and shells could not destroy these soft materials. Fort Sumter soon became a symbol of Southern resistance.

When the approach of Sherman's army forced Confederate troops to leave Charleston in February, 1865, Fort Sumter again became the property of the United States. It was Major General Robert Anderson who was given the honor of hoisting over the fort the same flag that he had lowered just four years before. His voice filled with emotion as he said, "I thank God that I have lived to see this day, and to be here, to perform this, perhaps the last act of my life, of duty to my country."

☆ In 1948, Fort Sumter became a national monument. Its
☆ crumbling shell at war's end has been restored and is
☆ now administered by the National Park Service.

FORT DONELSON

"No terms except an unconditional and immediate surrender can be accepted. I propose to move immediately upon your works." With these gruff words, Brigadier General Ulysses S. Grant claimed the Union's first major victory of the Civil War. It was February 1862 and Fort Donelson had fallen.

A month earlier in Washington, President Abraham Lincoln had grown more and more restless. After ten months of civil war, the North had achieved very little in its fight to save the Union. With the Confederates' sweeping victory at Manassas, Virginia (The Battle of Bull Run) in July, 1861, the South became a bit too cocky. The North, on the other hand, was jolted into serious effort.

Spoiling for a fight, Union commander Ulysses S. Grant eyed two fortifications, Forts Henry and Donelson which commanded the Tennessee and Cumberland Rivers. The Confederacy had built these earthen works to protect the center of their western line which stretched across northern Tennessee and southern Kentucky. Grant thought that if he could take these two forts, the pathway to the heartland of the Confederacy would be wide open. He was determined to succeed.

On February 6, Grant and his fleet commander, Flag
Officer Andrew H. Foote, launched a land and river attack on
Fort Henry. Nine transports, four ironclad gunboats and three
wooden vessels, ferried 15,000 soldiers up the rain-swollen
Tennessee River. Upon their arrival at the fort, Grant and
Foote discovered what the Confederate commander, Brigadier
General Lloyd Tilgham, knew all too well. Fort Henry was not
a fort in the true sense of the word. It could not be defended!

Built on low ground, the fort was nearly under water from
the rising Tennessee River when Foote's gunboats opened fire.
Trying valiantly to make the best of a bad situation, Tilgham
ordered most of his 2,600 men to flee to Fort Donelson about
12 miles (19 km) to the east. He and a small group of
artillerymen stayed behind to cover their withdrawal. The
Rebels battled remarkably well against impossible odds for
over an hour. They even managed to disable one of Foote's
gunboats. However, Tilghman soon saw that the situation was
hopeless and surrendered the little fort. The Navy had won the
duel alone before the infantry arrived on the scene. For while
the battle raged, Grant's troops had still been slogging through
the mud!

Feeling quite charmed, the victorious Union troops marched overland toward Fort Donelson. Even the sun seemed to smile down upon them as the harsh winter weather turned unusually warm and springlike. Along the way, the soldiers peeled off their heavy blue overcoats and threw them aside. Little did they think they would soon be shivering in their shirtsleeves in a blizzard of sleet and snow.

On February 13, Grant's forces launched an unsuccessful attack on Fort Donelson. That same evening bitter winter weather taunted the freezing troops for casting off their winter gear. The following day, Foote's gunboats bombarded the water batteries but were driven back by Rebel gunfire. The fleet suffered heavy damages and Foote, himself, was mortally wounded. Disappointed but not discouraged, Grant knew that this time, the Army alone must win the battle.

In the chilling dawn of February 15, the Rebel yell, a bloodcurdling shout, pierced the cold air. The Confederates attacked the numbed Yankees as they were rising from their icy bunks. As the Blue and the Gray struggled against each other, the Union army retreated. The Rebels had opened up an escape route but then failed to take advantage of it! The Confederate command had faltered at the wrong moment. Grant seized the opportunity! He counterattacked swiftly and drove the enemy back. Victory was his.

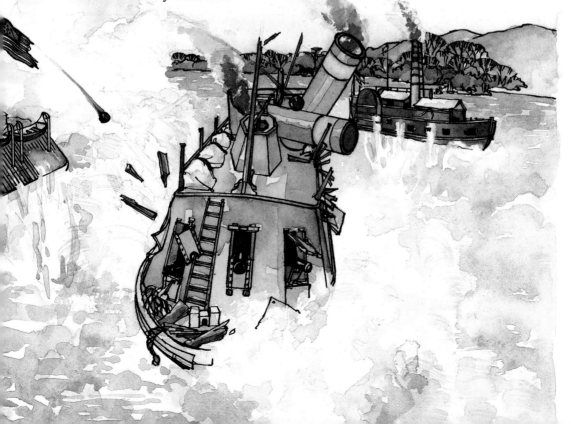

LEFT: General Ulysses Grant
RIGHT: General Simon Buckner
BELOW: Grant's demand for unconditional surrender

No terms except an unconditional and immediate surrender can be accepted. U. S. Grant

Inside the fort, the two ranking generals, John Floyd and Gideon Pillow, refused to surrender and become Yankee prisoners. Instead they turned over their command to Simon Buckner and slipped away. Buckner was not delighted. He had the difficult duty of asking fellow West Pointer Grant for terms of surrender. Despite the fact that Buckner had once made Grant a life-saving loan when he was down on his luck, Grant showed no mercy. A soldier to the core, Grant did not let personal affairs get in the way of military matters. He demanded unconditional and immediate surrender.

The important victories at Fort Henry and at Fort Donelson lifted the sagging spirits of the North. Moreover, the people now had the hero they had longed for—Unconditional Surrender Grant.

☆ Today Fort Donelson is a National Military Park and
☆ Cemetery. It is administered by the National Park
☆ Service. The earthworks, fort walls, outer defenses and
☆ water batteries still remain.

FORT PULASKI

After the War of 1812, the United States realized that its Atlantic and Gulf coastlines had to be strengthened against enemy invasion. No one could forget how easily British troops had sacked Washington and destroyed parts of the Middle Atlantic States. As a result, Congress set up a Board of Engineers to direct all phases of seacoast fortification design and construction for the whole country. General Simon Bernard, a French military engineer who had served under Napoleon, was selected to be in charge of the Board.

General Bernard made the first drafts for an immense fort to be built on Cockspur Island, where there had been two earlier forts, and construction began in 1829. Robert E. Lee began his famous military career working on the dikes and drainage system for the island from 1829 to 1831.

Building the brick structure was a gigantic project. Lieutenant Joseph Mansfield worked on the fort with unflagging devotion for many years. Despite many delays caused by disease, lack of money, hurricane gales and bitter wintery winds, Mansfield doggedly saw to the fort's completion in 1847. When it was finally finished, the five-sided fort was named for Count Casimir Pulaski, the Polish hero who gave his services and his life to America during the Revolutionary War.

By January 1861, the North and the South teetered on the brink of war. Shock and anger at the Federal Government's occupation of Fort Sumter in Charleston, South Carolina, rallied Georgians into action. In a fever of excitement, on January 3, 1861, Georgia troops led by Colonel Alexander R. Lawton seized Fort Pulaski before the Federals had a chance to send a garrison to defend it. Proudly whipping in the breeze, the Georgian flag defied the North to recapture the fort.

The following year the Union batteries led by General Quincy A. Gillmore gladly accepted the challenge. Under cover of darkness, Federal forces dragged guns, supplies and ammunition across the soft marshes of Tybee Island, a mile (less than 2 km) from Fort Pulaski's walls.

"Early yesterday morning a flag of truce came over from Tybee Island conveying a demand for the surrender of the fort. Of course I could give but one answer, that I was there to fight not to yield," so wrote Colonel Charles Olmstead to his wife. Once the Federal artillery thundered out, he and his Confederate soldiers tried desperately to defend the fort.

To their utter horror, they watched the Union's new rifled artillery rip great gaping holes in the fort's 2–4 yard (2–4 meter) thick masonry walls. Try as they might, Olmstead's loyal men in gray could not combat the tremendous power and accuracy of these new weapons. The fort that had cost a million dollars to build and was said to be as strong as the Rocky Mountains, crumbled before their very eyes! And so, after thirty hours of bombardment, the Confederates resisted no longer. With heavy hearts they lowered their flag, the Stars

and Bars, and replaced it with the white cloth of surrender. This siege clearly pointed out that even dense brick walls could not withstand rifled cannons. It marked the end of the era of moated forts.

After the fall of Fort Pulaski, it was manned by Federal troops. It became an important part of the economic blockade of the entire South.

☆
☆
☆   Thanks to the National Park Service which has carefully
☆   restored and preserved Fort Pulaski National Monu-
☆   ment, visitors are encouraged to stroll the grounds.
☆   They can inspect the fort's detailed brickwork, demi-
☆   bastions, wet moat, drawbridge and demilune and actu-
☆   ally see for themselves what it would be like to live in
☆   and defend a fort.

FORT JEFFERSON

Dr Samuel Mudd huddled in his dank dungeon. He wondered how he could possibly stand to spend the rest of his life in such a miserable place. He had been sentenced to life in prison at lonely Fort Jefferson for setting the broken leg of Abraham Lincoln's assassin, John Wilkes Booth. Unluckily, he had not known at the time that he was treating a criminal.

After two gloomy years of shackles and rotten food, Dr Mudd was given the chance to win his freedom. When a yellow fever epidemic swept through the fort in 1867, felling 270 of the 300-man garrison, Dr Mudd worked with great dedication to fight the awful disease. For his excellent work Mudd won a pardon and once again became a free man.

34

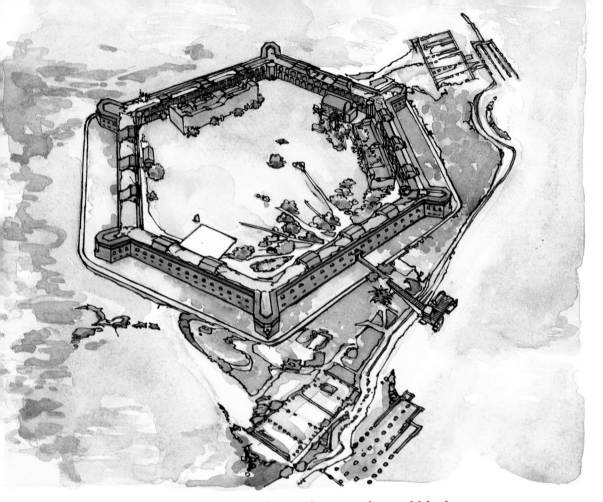

Fort Jefferson has not always been a place of bleakness and despair. Its location on Garden Key off the tip of Florida in the crystal waters of the Gulf of Mexico was first sighted by the Spanish explorer, Ponce de Leon, in 1513. Garden Key is one of a cluster of seven small, low islands made up of sand and coral. Ponce de Leon named these reefs Las Tortugas—The Turtles—after the large number of turtles he found there. The Tortugas served as a harbor for pirates in the centuries that followed.

In 1829 US Naval Lt Josiah Tattnall surveyed the islands and pointed out their strategic value. A growing nation must keep its shipping routes safe. If the Tortugas should fall into enemy hands, the Mississippi Valley commerce, which sailed the Gulf to reach the Atlantic Ocean, would be endangered. Because of this threat, the US War Department ordered the construction of Fort Jefferson on Garden Key. It was to become the largest link in the chain of seacoast forts from Maine to Texas.

Begun in 1846, construction on the enormous hexagonal fort continued for almost thirty years. The Corps of Engineers planned it to have three gun-tiers to hold 450 guns and to house 1,500 men. Northern artisans and Southern slaves labored to build the brick walls to a height of 50 feet (15 meters) and a thickness of 8 feet (2.5 meters). After the Emancipation Proclamation freed the slaves in 1863, military prisoners were sent to Garden Key to work on the fort. Despite years of toil, Fort Jefferson was never really finished.

But just because there was a lack of military action did not mean that the soldiers at Fort Jefferson had an easy time. Their meat rations spoiled in the scorching heat. They often tasted salt, seaweed and insects in their bread. Fresh fruits and vegetables were in very short supply. Even the rain water they had to collect for drinking water frequently turned brackish. On top of all these hardships, the men also had to live with isolation, the boredom of daily routine and the constant menace of disease.

Finally, in 1874, the Army abandoned Fort Jefferson. It was later used briefly as a naval base, a seaplane base and as one of the first naval wireless stations. In 1935, President Franklin D. Roosevelt named the area a national monument.

☆ Today tourists and campers can visit Garden Key by
☆ boat or by seaplane. Here they can study the fascinating
☆ marine life of the clear, turquoise waters and tour the
☆ proud old fort that was called the Gibraltar of the Gulf.
☆ So what was once a desolate prison to some is now a
☆ tropical paradise to many, administered by the National
☆ Park Service.

FORT POINT

High on a chalky white cliff at the entrance to San Francisco Bay, stood a Spanish fort built of adobe, or sun-dried bricks, in 1794. The site had been chosen nearly two decades earlier as the ideal place for a presidio (military post) by Colonel Juan Bautista de Anza. After Anza went back to Mexico and colonization was underway, however, it was decided that Anza's choice would make a better spot for a coastal fortification. As a result, the Presidio of San Francisco was established about a mile (1.5 km) southeast of the white cliff. The little fort, El Castillo De San Joaquin, became the property of Mexico when she became free of Spanish rule.

El Castillo had many flaws. The thick walls quivered and crumbled whenever the guns were fired. Even the cannons were poorly mounted. Howling storms and earthquakes often caused major damage. Finally, in 1835, the Mexican garrison moved north and abandoned the fort.

During the Mexican War, California fell into American hands in 1847. That same year, American troops were stationed at the Presidio. But with the discovery of gold at Sutter's Mill in California, many soldiers could not resist the promise of sudden wealth and bolted for the gold fields. The lure of gold was to change San Francisco from a sleepy port to a rich and famous city.

A board of engineer officers advised that a strong fort be built at the El Castillo site to protect the great landlocked harbor from hostile fleets. Major (later General) J. G. Barnard started the project in 1853.

The old Spanish fortress and the high white bluff on which it perched were leveled to make way for the new structure, Fort Point. The site had to be closer to water level so that modern artillery could be used to full advantage.

Fort Point was under construction until 1861. Its plan somewhat resembles that of Fort Sumter in South Carolina. It is in the shape of an irregular rectangle. There are two spurs, or bastions, protruding from the northeast and northwest corners. The fort's thick brick walls enclose a parade (courtyard), which is surrounded on three sides facing the water with galleries of tiered brick arches. Here, situated one above the other are three tiers of gun ports. Above these tiers is a fourth tier of guns, the barbette tier, which covered the approaches from both land and sea. At one time nearly 130 guns were mounted on these four tiers.

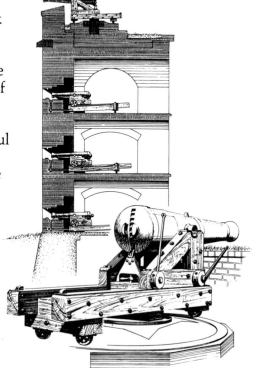

Perhaps the most remarkable feature of Fort Point is the artful stone work of the master masons who worked on the fort. The hand-cut brick arches and the three spiral staircases made of solid granite slabs are architectural marvels.

In fact the fort's masterful construction saved it from destruction. Around 1930 the fort was doomed to be demolished to make way for the Golden Gate Bridge. Joseph B. Strauss, the chief engineer for the bridge project, refused to allow such an impressive structure to be torn down. Instead he designed an enormous steel arch to span the fort.

During the Civil War, Fort Point stood armed and ready to defend the Union. However, no Confederate ships ventured into the Bay. So at the War's end, not a single shot had been fired by the fort.

Even the violent trembling of the earth during the dreadful San Francisco Earthquake in 1906 did very little damage to Fort Point. Army troops from the fort and the Presidio helped to keep order and to give out food and water to the victims of the earthquake.

When the United States was plunged into World War II, Fort Point again answered the call to serve the nation. After the surprise attack by the Japanese on Pearl Harbor on December 7, 1941, Americans feared that the Pacific Coast might be the next target. Soldiers were ordered to the fort to defend San Francisco Bay. As their bright searchlights scanned the skies, the troops were prepared to fight off the enemy with anti-aircraft guns. A submarine net stretched across the entrance to the Bay to stop submarines from slipping in to attack.

☆ Due to the foresight of Joseph B. Strauss and to the
☆ devoted efforts of the Fort Point and Army Museum
☆ Association, the magnificent fort is a National Historic
☆ Site today. It is managed by the National Park Service.
☆ To visit Fort Point is to learn a lesson on the greatness
☆ of America.

THE ALAMO

In the beginning the Alamo was only a humble mission. Today it is a hallowed shrine to one of the most heroic struggles in all of history. Called the "Cradle of Texas Liberty," the Alamo symbolizes extreme courage and bravery.

As more and more people from the United States settled in Texas, they longed for independence from Mexico. When the Texas Revolution started, the Mexican military used the Alamo in San Antonio as headquarters. In December 1835 Texas revolutionaries captured the fortified mission. Commander-in-chief Sam Houston warned that the Mexicans would return. He advised that the Alamo should be demolished and abandoned. His superiors had a different view. The Alamo must be held.

On February 23, 1836, Houston's prediction came true. Mexican leader Antonio de Santa Anna and some 6,000 men entered San Antonio. Inside the Alamo's mouldering walls, Colonels William B. Travis and James Bowie commanded a pitifully small garrison of some 150 fighting men. Davy Crockett, the well-known backwoodsman from Tennessee was

among them. They knew they faced certain doom against such overwhelming numbers. Yet, when Santa Anna demanded immediate surrender, they answered boldly with a cannon shot. The Mexican attackers then hoisted the blood red flag of "no quarter;" this meant that no mercy would be shown.

Legend has it that Travis drew a line in the dirt with the tip of his sword. He challenged his men to cross over the line if they were willing to stay and fight to their death. Every member of that plucky little band stepped over the fateful mark. Even Bowie who had fallen ill insisted that he be carried across in his sickbed!

Reinforced by 32 more men who had scrambled through enemy lines, Travis and his stouthearted followers braved Santa Anna's legions. The final assault took place on March 6, the thirteenth day of battle. As the bugles blared the *Degüello* (meaning "no quarter"), the Mexicans stormed the Alamo on all sides. Suffering dreadful losses, the attackers succeeded in scaling the walls. The siege ended in hand-to-hand combat in the courtyard and buildings. Even Bowie fought from his cot. But at the battle's end, every defender was dead.

"Remember the Alamo!" cried Houston. The massacre aroused the fighting wrath of all Texans. Six weeks later they soundly defeated Santa Anna's army at San Jacinto. Texas was free!

FORT LARAMIE

Fur-trapping brought the need for the first fort on the Laramie, on the eastern prairies of what is now Wyoming. In the early 1800s, garments made from beaver fur were very fashionable. Eager trappers flocked to Laramie River country where beaver were plentiful. Seeing the opportunity to make a profit from the region, two fur traders, William Sublette and Robert Campbell, founded a trading post on the Laramie in 1834. This log stockade fort, named Fort William, after Sublette, was generally known as "Fort Laramie."

After this post had passed into the hands of the American Fur Company in 1836, it quickly became one of the chief trading centers in the Rocky Mountains. The fort was a lively scene as buckskin-clad traders and Indians bartered for goods. Camping outside the walls of the fort, bands of Sioux, Cheyenne and Arapahoe brought pelts and buffalo robes to trade for dry goods, knives, tobacco, colored beads, bright cloth and whiskey. Fur traders, as well, relied heavily on Fort Laramie for their supplies and for protection against unfriendly Indians.

By 1841, Fort William's cottonwood walls had begun to rot. The American Fur Company replaced the decaying old fort with a sturdier structure built of adobe. Although this new fort was christened Fort John, everyone still called it Fort Laramie.

The second Fort Laramie also was a stockade fort with blockhouses at two of the corners. A small wooden fence, or palisade, rested on top of the 16-foot (5-meter) high walls as an extra defense against attackers. Close to the inside walls were small cabins. This design made it possible for people to stand on the cabin rooftops and fire over the stockade during times of siege.

By 1842, fur trading as an industry was suffering. Mountain men had been much too successful in their tracking, trapping and trading. As a result, the once abundant supply of beaver was nearly gone. The rugged trappers were forced to venture into new territory in search of the beaver. However, even when they did manage to find enough pelts to sell, the prices they could sell them for were very low. What had been worth six dollars in 1832 could barely fetch one dollar just ten years later! For fashion is often fickle and beaver fur was no longer popular. Stylish people had shifted their attention to other materials.

By no means did the failing fur business spell the end of Fort Laramie. As the nation expanded westward, thousands upon thousands of weary emigrants paused at this fort on the Oregon Trail for mail, supplies and repairs. Brigham Young and his company of Mormons stopped here in 1847 while on their way to a new life in Utah. By 1849 thousands of gold-

seekers and pioneers were trekking to California. Countless
covered wagons rolled along the deeply rutted road into Fort
Laramie where their passengers sought relief from the hardships
of a long journey. Hardly a westbound traveler did not know
Fort Laramie.

The United States Government bought Fort Laramie from
the trading company in 1849 for $4,000. The government
erected many new buildings and Fort Laramie became a
military post. For many years the fort's mission was to restrain
Indians in their desperate bids to keep their lands. It was the
headquarters for many military campaigns.

Several important treaties were signed at Fort Laramie.
The Sioux, Cheyenne and other tribes of the Great Plains
surrendered most of their claims to the region in exchange for
money.

Fort Laramie even shared in the excitement of the Pony
Express. Lightweight riders carrying sacks of mail galloped into
the fort which was one of the stations along the way. In only
two minutes, they tossed their saddlebags over fresh ponies
and sped off again in a whirl of dust.

By 1890 the American frontier had come to a close. Fort
Laramie's long days of service were at an end. The garrison
marched out of the old post never to return.

 Fort Laramie is now a National Historic Site administered by the National Park Service. Once again it wel-
comes visitors.

FORT SMITH

Many modern North American cities can trace their roots back to early forts. Fort Smith, Arkansas, is such a city.

It all began in 1817 when Major William Bradford and a company of the United States Rifle Regiment built a small log and stone stockade on high ground overlooking the junction of the Arkansas and Poteau Rivers. The army fortified this site, now known as Belle Pointe, to restore peace between the feuding Osage and Cherokee Indians. They named the fort in honor of General Thomas A. Smith, commander of all Federal forces west of the Mississippi River. In those days it was a common practice to name western forts after army officers.

After Osage and Cherokee chiefs agreed to the terms set forth in the 1822 Treaty of Fort Smith, most of the differences between the two nations were settled. As the Arkansas frontier became quieter, the troops at Fort Smith battled boredom. Being soldiers, they much preferred the rugged adventures of patrolling to the dull routine of garrison housekeeping. To their relief, they received orders to abandon the post in 1824. The little fort soon lay in ruins.

After President Andrew Jackson took office in 1829, the government pressed even harder to push eastern Indians westward. The Cherokees who were forced to give up their land in Georgia and move to Oklahoma called their long, sad journey the Trail of Tears. Heartbroken over leaving their homeland, over 15,000 men, women and children traveled mostly on foot under the worst possible conditions. Many did not survive the ordeal.

Upset by the swelling numbers of Indians who came to the region as a result of Jackson's "Indian Removal" policy,

Arkansas settlers asked the government for protection. In 1838, the army began construction on a large permanent fortification within view of the first Fort Smith. The second Fort Smith had two officers' quarters, a barracks, and commissary and quartermaster storehouses, all enclosed by a stone wall. Eventually, the fort found a role other than defense. It became a thriving depot, supplying such necessities as mules, wagons, uniforms and weapons to military posts farther west.

Fort Smith's most famous era began after the army finally left in 1871 and Judge Isaac C. Parker of the Western District of Arkansas moved in. He came to bring law and order to the raw Indian Territory which had become a haven for thieves and thugs of the worst sort. Judge Parker let it be known far and wide that his court would not be soft on criminals. Law-breakers soon realized he meant what he said!

This stern but fair man was called the "hanging judge" and for good reason. During his 21 years at Fort Smith, he heard more than 13,000 cases and sent 79 men to the gallows. He and his 200 United States Deputy Marshals worked hard and at great personal risk to see that justice was done.

 Today the National Park Service maintains Fort Smith National Historic Site which includes the remains of both forts and the Federal Court for the Western District of Arkansas.